A story Jesus told

Are you good at listening?

LOTS of people listened to Jesus.
He told us about God's love for us
and how to love God and other people.

Some people LISTENED to what Jesus said,

Everyone who listens to me,
 AND does what I say, is like a clever man

who built his house on big, **STRONG** rocks.

splosh,

POUR!

still.

Phew!
Those GREAT BIG rocks
made it strong.

But Jesus said, "Anyone who listens to me, but does NOT do what I say,

is like a silly man ...

who built his house on soft, loose sand.
Uh oh!

If we don't care about what God says, we end up in a terrible mess.

Notes for grown-ups

Jesus taught the crowds how to follow God and love others. Some people seemed to listen and called him their "Lord", yet they did not really care about doing what God wants and did not do what Jesus taught. He said that when these people expect to be welcomed into God's world in heaven, he will tell them he never knew them. (This is in Matthew 7 v 21-23.) After saying this, Jesus told this story about the two builders, who, he said, represent those who listen and respond to his words, and those who listen but don't do anything in response.

So what does it mean to listen to Jesus and do what he said? We have all shown the attitudes that Jesus said break God's laws—such as anger, selfishness and pride—and we all fail to follow his teaching perfectly. When we hear Jesus' teaching on what it means to truly love others, the right response is to recognise that our lives don't measure up to this, to come to God for forgiveness, and to ask for his help to live with him as the real King in our lives—as Jesus taught that we should.

To think that we are fine as we are, or to say that we believe in God without it having an effect on our lives, is like building a house on the sand. But if we genuinely want to follow God, we will want to live the way Jesus teaches, trusting in God's help and forgiveness. This will show in our actions, not just in words, and we will have the rock-solid security of a real relationship with God.

Matthew 7 v 24-27
(The Bible: New International Version)

[Jesus said,] 24 "Therefore everyone who hears these words of mine and puts them into practice is like a wise man who built his house on the rock. 25 The rain came down, the streams rose, and the winds blew and beat against that house; yet it did not fall, because it had its foundation on the rock. 26 But everyone who hears these words of mine and does not put them into practice is like a foolish man who built his house on sand. 27 The rain came down, the streams rose, and the winds blew and beat against that house, and it fell with a great crash."

Little me BIG GOD

Collect the series

- The Man Who Would Not Be Quiet • Never Too Little • The Best Thing To Do
- The Dad Who Never Gave Up • The Boy Who Shared His Sandwich
- The Easter Fix • The Little Man Whose Heart Grew Big
- How Can I Pray? • The House That Went Splat • The Christmas Surprise

The House That Went Splat
© Stephanie Williams, 2022. Reprinted 2022, 2023.

Published by:
The Good Book Company

thegoodbook.com | thegoodbook.co.uk
thegoodbook.com.au | thegoodbook.co.nz | thegoodbook.co.in

Unless indicated, all Scripture references are taken from the Holy Bible, New International Version. Copyright © 2011 Biblica. Used by permission.

Stephanie Williams has asserted her right under the Copyright, Designs and Patents Act 1988 to be identified as the author and illustrator of this work.

All rights reserved. Except as may be permitted by the Copyright Act, no part of this publication may be reproduced in any form or by any means without prior permission from the publisher.

ISBN: 9781784987565 | JOB-007403 | Printed in India